Terry Cree is a writer and artist who lives in Hampshire. He has run a sculpture park, designed a number of gardens, organized poetry readings by many of the most significant names in post-war British poetry and has taught English and creative writing to countless numbers of young people and adults.

Fruit

Terry Cree

TWO
RIVERS
PRESS

First published in the UK in 2014 by Two Rivers Press
7 Denmark Road, Reading RG1 5PA.
www.tworiverspress.com

ISBN 978-1-901677-97-3

1 2 3 4 5 6 7 8 9

Two Rivers Press is represented in the UK by Inpress Ltd and
distributed by Central Books.

Cover painting, self-portrait and drawings by Terry Cree.
Typeset in Janson and Parisine.

Printed and bound in Great Britain by Imprint Digital, Exeter.

For Lorna, Elissa, Sam and Alix

*Special thanks to Adrian Blamires for his friendship
and encouragement*

Contents

Fruit

Josephine Jones

In a tent of clouds
I am six years old
in Mercer's Field
in the burning air,

with the broomrape
and the quaking grass
and the hurrying beetle
and the centipede

and Josephine Jones,
who was five years old,
for whom my tent of
clouds and sky was made.

And in that hot field,
with the sun roaring
and the earth still,
I learned to be alone,

not only alone as
in the ticking hour
when starlings peck
the yard and fly away

but a new alone,
surprising as the
sudden rush for dark
beneath a lifted stone.

Josephine had flowers
on her heart, and hands
that could tie in chains
for love the day's eyes.

She blew and scattered
all in one bold breath
the grey dandelion
just to know the time.

My airy tent was
nothing new to her,
who knew what she knew
and did not care.

Two was more alone
than one, and sage
Josephine Jones
liked it that I knew.

She was the dark cleft
I will carry with me
till the raging sun
falls out of the sky

and her sing-song hum
as she weaved her chains
is the indifference
I have tried to catch

and keep for myself
in a field of my own
with the similes that
later came to me.

Meatyard Triptypch

Wer zeigt ein Kind, so wie es steht?

1

The children frozen in the yard
Have stopped their play to be looked at.
Theirs is a serious game that
Is all about trying too hard.

Barthes called cameras "clocks for seeing".
These children have another sense
Of time. They have the perfect tense
For standing still to be caught in.

If you ask them to occupy
Your recreation with a look,
What they contrive to give you back
May be cold murder through the eye.

*

Optician turned photographer
From Normal, Illinois, his life
Was mostly Madelyn, his wife,
His sons, Michael and Christopher,

Melissa, his daughter, and these,
Arranged in various poses,
Often in abandoned houses,
Were his subject, along with trees,

Zen configurations of twig,
No-focus photographs, portraits,
Light on water shots, self-portraits,
Pictures of love, abstractions – big

Ideas, but at the same time just
A man recording how his kids
Grew up. He arranged them amidst
Pipes, leaves, tangles of branches, messed

Up residues of lives long gone,
The abandonment of history,
Or out in the open where he
Gave them the space to be alone.

The face is often difficult
To read, sometimes blurred, sometimes set
To express some purposeful thought
At odds with the easily felt.

This is particularly so
Of the children. What does it mean
When a child by its yawn or lean
Into another seems to know

More than we imagine they do?
Was it his intention to make
Us feel that way, to make us take
A view of what is here shot through

With the cold insolence of thought,
The child remote and uncaring
Of what the adult mind staring
Through the camera thinks it ought?

The way that he arranges them
In space in secretive clusters
Or wilfully alone confers
Upon their thoughts a stratagem

To undermine that old pretence
To primal innocence. Their minds
Are not amenable. What winds
With them along a barbed-wire fence

Or through a shuttered room pasted
With rose swags or vines, or under
Some graffito meant to render
Love's eternity, now wasted,

Is that seriousness of mind
That sees itself at play and knows
That playing should not presuppose
A simple nature unrefined.

Here's a child sitting in a field
Of demolition with the Stars
And Stripes and a dead doll. And here's
Another with its face concealed

Behind a shard of glass, and here,
Sitting in the sassafras, two
More, one with his dark face askew,
The other face-on but a blur,

Kids doing what the adults do,
Playing at life until a sense
Of self emerges from the chance
Contrivances they're shaping to.

Meatyard turns them into smudges,
Crucified ghosts hung on the air,
Emanations in the grass where
Buildings fold with age, images

That always comprehend the space
The subject moves in and the way
They move. Time is never very
Far away. Dereliction's pace

Is set against the tumbling rush
Of kids who'd like to hurry it
Along. Paint peels and clapboards split,
Floors are flooded, windows are smashed,

And in the midst of this the kids
Are spectrally themselves, booming
And rolling through the days, aiming
At nothing special, doing Dad's

Bidding by miming the paint splash
Drip-dried on the wall behind them.
Give him what he wants and then some.
That black premonitory gash

In the plaster, for example
Like some dark angel hovering,
That the boy in white is turning
To peruse, is uncomfortable

To look at not because its spread
Recalls our yawning birth - Earth's door
Screaming on its hinges - but more
Because its webbed wings are echoed

In the tightened folds in the boy's
Jeans and in the congruent hands-
In-pockets slouch. The way he stands
With his head lost in blur conveys

His shifty interest in the hole
That lies beyond the corner crease
Where wall meets wall. This loss of face
Is Meatyard's ace. A peeling wall

Provides more clues than faces do.
Faces are evasions. The lens
Cannot convey a proper sense
Of what a person is, or who.

He seemed to get this early on,
In Georgetown Street, where black kids scowl
Or laugh and look away, and all
The eye need know is spattered on

The wall they lean against – dimpling,
Grey percussion marks from missiles
Fired to erase the painted smiles
Of whitey wives, set on sampling

The favoured lives they advertise.
Nothing in those children's faces
Tells the story like the places
And the hours living occupies.

The faces frown, avert their eyes.
The camera shoots but cannot
Take the life of what is shot.
It's an auditor of old lies,

Of necessary excuses,
Embarrassed denials, not who
We are. It's true to the not true,
Catching less than it loses.

For Meatyard things are all we know –
Scythes, pump handles, fallen sashes,
Upturned boats, paint cans and ashes –
Everything we make and let go

The kids absorb into their game.
Theirs is the dash to use and know
Before they know too well. The slow
Involuntary pace of time

In things as they rot on a wall
Will be something for later on.
For now, Dad, try to catch your son
As he races blurred through it all,

Like a river through a canyon
Where the trees reaching for the light
Know only to grow and the white
Sky knows only to carry on.

2

Lucybelle Crater has a friend
Whose name is Lucybelle Crater.
We'll all know sooner or later
How the whole thing is going to end

And LC knows too and has brought
Her family and friends to see
How brave Murcan courage can be
And how far words alone fall short.

*

You ask your much-loved wife to pose
In a rubber hag's mask and age.
You make her open like a page
In her white sneakers and black hose

Which, I suppose, in some way stand
For the black-and-white you shoot in
But also your own death and mourning
And the old need to understand.

This family album that you made
Is all about that setting out,
The need to say before you get
Beyond the point of what is said.

Everyone agreed to be shot,
Hiding whatever other thought
They had behind the same shop-bought
Masquerade, so that only what

The body said or where it stood
Within its square expressed a view.
At the start and at the end you
Placed yourself with her, to make good

As well as anybody could
The damage of the loss to come.
You framed like brackets the whole dumb
Ache of severance of the blood,

Once as yourself and once as her,
Leaning in to kiss, with your ring
Shining on the hand that's resting
On him/her, in the grape arbor.

And it's part of the echoing
Of image against image here
That your framing shots commandeer
Two trees and two poles, following

The Fall, I think, and the two trees
Found in Paradise. There's a snake
Of hose coiling at your feet back
At the start, and I guess that these

Grapevines also follow Christian
Typology – *I am the vine,*
You are my branches – as a sign
That this is not all. The question

Of belief when one is dying
Finds its measure in tropes like this.
Whether or not eternal bliss
Emerges from our fevered doing,

The fact is final works touch deep.
And knowing this you organize
Your people, posing them in twos,
To give them something fixed to keep.

You make a set of sixty-four –
The sixth power of two and the squares
On a chess board. There are no spares
Or singletons. Everything here

Inclines to be a pair. LC
Herself (your lovely Madelyn
Unmasked) is always coupled in
These frames. Perhaps you meant to say

To her that that would be OK,
That doubles are the way of things.
A woman left alone soon longs
For coupling. What these pairs convey

To me, though, is the range of ways
It's possible to be beside
Another. Gestures may elide
Into the genitive of days

Most of the time but side-by-side
Has privileged significance
When posed. The Arnolfini once
Knew this as did the lazy-eyed,

Tied-back Ma of "American
Gothic". We pose, and the sharp eye
Of the camera asks of us why
We've stopped still? The best that we can

Answer most of the time is that
Occasion gave us pause. We stopped
To say about ourselves, inept
In these dark matters mostly, that

This is how we'd like to be seen.
Let it be recorded that I,
Lucybelle Crater, have an eye
For the significance of known

Things reendowed with proper sense
After all the years lost on them –
Swing set, Bible, irises, hem
Line, clothes line, cuts of spruce, the dense,

Dim cacophony of daily
Items suddenly made solemn
By the presage of death in them.
Let me be taken here, fully

Myself and fully the other;
That's to say, quotidian me
And me unmasked, the person free
To be posed, the wife, the lover.

There's that old pale presentiment
Shaking the grass. It's in the trees
Too with their attitudes, the ways
The wind makes them sturdy or bent.

Now death takes my picture and I,
On the other side of the lens,
Do as I'm told. What soon will once
Have been his wife I give the eye

That knows me - my body in its
Usual pose, my attitude,
My awkwardness. I am a nude
In clothes. I am the face that fits

The mask. I'm Lucybelle Crater
And this is how I face the day,
Sitting on a see-saw the way
He wants me to, the relater

Of my life, my look-see husband.
Let him expose me, let him hide
Me in a mask. Let him confide
The mystery of me to the hand

That turns the page. I will be known
Only to the few who know me.
The rest have only what they see.
And when he's gone, the children grown,

This family album that he made
To make connection with us all
Will lie upon my lap and call
Up images of how we played,

Being and not being who we are,
And it will not be what we knew
Nor anything like, but the few
Who knew us will not really care.

3

Among the many that I love
This one of a boy, chin cradled
In his hands in thought, the head held
Like Munch's screaming head just above

The skyline, where it makes a three –
The nub of head, a little off-
Centre a pole, holding aloft
Two cable arms, and a young tree,

Fresh in leaf, I'd say, which divides
In two the space between the pole
And the left edge of the frame while
Standing in counterpoise besides

With the boy, so that the two weigh
Equally and balance the shot.
The boy, we see at last, is squat
On a head that's facing our way.

Singer Sargent did something like
This in his picture of the Boit
Girls, placing a baby doll tight
Between the youngest's legs to make

A generative point as each
In age receded into shade.
(So lives are lost as they are made
And day by day grow out of reach.)

The head the boy is sitting on
Is from a female manikin;
The tree implies, perhaps, old sin
Grown fresh, the pole Christ's redemption,

And the boy, not unreasonably,
Has much to think about in this.
The empty space of new-mown grass
He occupies so pensively

With its mow lines receding to
The point that the Golden Section
Demands should mark the division
Of earth and sky, not leading to

Infinity but thus curtailed,
This empty space that's free of shade
Except where the boy's face is hid
Is a kind of putative world,

Stripped down as Beckett would have done.
Around the pole and tree, unmown,
There is a rough raggedy zone
Of longer grass. That apart, none

Of the components of the scene
Show any trace of variance.
The sky is uniformly dense
With pallid blanket cloud and, seen

Against this, the pole betrays its
Slight unevenness. Once a tree
Itself, a lodgepole pine maybe,
Imported from the Western States,

It has, in spite of being turned,
The sense to wander from the true.
In the wet mountains where it grew
The high light to which its tip turned

Was not remote enough to make
For perfect uniformity.
Some wiggle to shake itself free
Of the rest is there in the quake

Rippling in its length, and the wire
It upholds echoes this in twists.
The boy by his thinking insists
There's a puzzle to be solved here,

The focus of which is nearly
Hidden in the grass at his feet –
A flask or two, catching the light? –
Something certainly, not clearly

Shown but hinting at the boy's thought –
Atilt, ectoplasmic, a vial
Of concentration, frosted, pale,
That might be everything, or not.

And then there's the head, looking out
Between his legs, her eyebrows arched
In beautified surprise, untouched
Otherwise, superior doubt

As to the possibilities
The one expression that she has.
She takes no notice of the glass
That hides her chin – something of his

That has its tip close to her lips
But not enough to hold her thought.
She looks like a boy herself, caught
Like some memory the mind grips

To itself not to be alone
At night, a face that half recalls
A dozen individuals,
Embracing all but never known.

If it's the mother of the boy
Implied it's as a young, gamine
Version of herself. Set between
His legs her painted hair sits by

His undeveloped groin. The rest
Of her is underground (or just
Detachable) as if she's lost
In loving all her interest,

Become a thing the children sit
Upon distracted. In the same
Shoot Meatyard moves us on in time.
The boy has had enough of it.

He slopes off with head sunk towards
The dead pole on the horizon,
But the sapling tree there has gone
And in its place further forward

A triangle of pubic pine
Implies a new thought that the doll
Hitched to the boy's back might compel.
The woman's head is set in line

With the thick coniferous V
And, sprouting by her head, a hand
That seems to be the wrong way round
Makes an O enigmatically.

Clouds are gathering in the sky
And there's a loss here that, for me,
Is instinct with the missing tree
And what its missing might imply.

In his final year Meatyard leaves
Some pictures of himself mounting
A ridge not unlike this. Standing
Beside him, a tree without leaves

Scratches the sky. He has lost weight,
His hair is gray, his face somehow
Simian, and the here and now
Is a backward look. Laid in wait,

He looks down the lens of himself,
Disposed on a bank, half-hidden
By the tangle of grass. Saddened,
Low, tousled as the turf, his health

A mess, Meatyard looks down on us,
And, in doing so, looks by chance
Like me. Only the circumstance
Of death, it seems to me, sets us

Apart. He has that doubtful look
I cast upon my own image
Whenever I'm stopped on a ridge
On my own, knowing what it took

To get there. He knows the prospect
And he knows the past and he sees
Beyond the evidence of trees
An empty, rolling land, exact

In its indifference to love.
The fingers of the tree beside
Him strain to get themselves inside
Some question falling from above

And we are low in the long grass
With the eyes in our empty heads
Looking up. So the earth embeds
Us in itself. It's no great loss.

Redemption lies in how to place
Figure beside figure and thing
Beside thing. And calculating
How a fingered O and a face

Careless of the world, eloquent
Of nothing in itself, convey
A loss as white as the long day
When a boy walks away intent

Upon some interest of his own
Is genius, I think; as when,
Later in life, the boy made man
Rises, turns, and goes on alone.

Flat Calm

The grocers and their groceries are gone.
Their nouns stand empty like minor saints' feast days.
Their brown-coated, once solicitous ghosts
Don't even bother to litter the streets.

The order boy's bicycle that blundered
Up the hill like a half-bagged buffalo
Is gone. Its jellied brawn and breaded hams
Gave out on the rough road to delivery.

The haberdashers, milliners and mercers
Are vanished like the nap beneath their hands;
The chandlers with their gauges and their grades,
Their braided hemp and coir, all coiled and waxed,

Their slow, deliberate trade; the woven sacks
Of cereals and beans, hefted and stacked
In soft ziggurats like the grain stores of Ur,
Like wrinkled grey provisions of the brain;

The hardware bins of ovals, pins and tacks,
The four-square probity of weathering wood,
The mottled ledgers of the warehousemen,
Their sharpened pencils licked and poised to tick

Like supervisory angels – all the stock takes
Of that clean and orderly imagined past
Line up in the mind in blue feint rows
Of perpetuity, like waves on which,

Beyond erosion and the ragged edge,
Precautionary voices rise and fall –
Shannon, Rockall, Malin, Hebrides,
Bailey, Fair Isle, Faeroes, Southeast Iceland.

The Consolation of Walls

I hope he found some consolation in walls. I almost think he did.

There is a wall inside me against which
I have been kicking a small rubber ball
                For years.

Sometimes it rolls back flat along the ground.
Sometimes it bounces back like feelings plotted
                On a graph,

That old oscillation of up and down.
I can't decide if it's the motive force
                Of ball

Bouncing against wall I feel in feeling
Or whether it's the stoical resistance
                Of that

Stonewall part of me that never submits.
And which is better, moving ball or wall?
                For now,

Like Mr Jellyby, I'll settle for
The cool consolation of a wall against
                My brow.

The ball can rest inside me like a stone,
As hard and rubbery as death, unkicked,
                Unthrown.

Cracked Ice

(After the two-fold screen by Maruyama Okyo in The British Museum)

Imagine not white exactly
But something like the whey that mist
Makes in the morning on a lake.

You are on that lake and the ice
Underfoot has started to crack.
Time runs away, not crazed or abstract

But clear as clock hands and exact.
You sip your green tea from a bowl.
Time runs away. Dark waits beneath.

And whereas in the West what we
Call the vanishing point is shown
Converging sharply to its end

With all the promise of a road
Concentred on some destiny
That ending wishes for itself,

Here the zigzag that will kill you
Vanishes half way and what's beyond
Is like the light you hoped to see

As it presents itself through paper,
Not white exactly but opaque,
Like morning mist upon a lake.

Old Roses

Mottisfont in late May, bud burst,
bee snuffle and brimstones,
orchids on the verge, the sun's
hot thumbs fumbling in the folds
of Madame Alfred Carrière,
Albertine and Maiden's Blush.
Another week or so and all the coach
tour coteries of old rosarians
will hie them here like bees
to stick their noses in the roses,
older women mostly, lingering
in that reverie of scent,
mute, stern and unconfiding,
every sense intent upon
the parting of those puckered lips
that blow and swell to fattening hips.

Sea Song

It is I who live my life as the double of the other

a man with something on his mind
stands on the seashore, looking out –

he likes the waves, the way they roll
up from a swell and slap the land

indolently, the way they fizz
and splash the rocks and then retire

into themselves, and he wonders
if a wave can have identity,

whether one wave is entity
unto itself or whether waves

are merely gestures of the sea,
antics in an endless game

of come and go, of tap and run –
he sees himself thinking these things

along the sea front, looking out
like Ishmael, and a portion

of his life lists from the main
towards sadness, as if sadness

were an island he occupies
already, out beyond the line

of the horizon, and the sea
the grey thought that apprehends it –

he imagines how it would be
to be deserted, not for now

only but perpetually,
and a corresponding feeling

like a wave heaps up inside him
to inundate the emptiness

engendering it – it carries him
towards that place in mind where all

the world's denied except that piece
on which he stands, looking outwards

overseas towards that other self,
the one who knows his loneliness –

he listens to the waves' lapping
lines, their motherly insistence

as they wash the rocks, wearing down
whatever knocks the rocks have known

with soothing surf – a surge of liquid
consolation fills his thinking –

he weighs his loneliness the way
the waves weigh the rocks, slippery

in their wet hands – does that island
man who knows his loneliness feel

the swell of pity ever, or is
he so tight on his own island

that others' lives matter no more
to him than sand on the seafloor?'

is he all need and appetite?
are the impenetrable depths

a meal for him and nothing more?
along the shore he stands upon

the grey flotsam of others floats
in the rock pools, the discarded

congregations of the tattered
and uprooted, each successive

wave bothering their tendency
to float into each other's space –

sticks and shards, fish-nibbled, wave-worn
and almost lost in the backwash,

a dark debris that jitters on
the surface of the little pools –

it wants to be a metaphor
for something lost but not dismissed,

but to the thought attending to
its bitty, wave-tossed agitation

it isn't that at all – just the
persistence of old suffering

bobbing on the margins of the
placid mind – why remember it?

and all the while the endless waves
set their thoughts out on the shoreline –

this is how it is – this is it
for sure – one truth on another,

each one rolling out its failing
froth over the previous one's

gasping retreat, and to the man
on the seafront it's all one thing –

a sea of opinion, grasping
for the elusive rocks like drowning –

he sees his other self alone
on his island, untouched by waves,

irritated even by the
endless cycle of assertion

and denial – even the rocks
are powerless to make a stand –

their worried brows awash with waves,
their old foundations buried in sand –

and though the waves are said by some
to sigh as they die, their sighing

signals nothing to our lonely
man except the limits of love,

his own heartfelt perimeter,
where wasted words won't wash again –

his eyes are fixed on the horizon,
that other line that draws a fine

distinction on this layered earth –
folding, unfolding, refolding

itself, the sea subtends all points
within its shifting surfaces,

like Nash's winter sea that plots
within its scalene waves the fins

and grounded wings of Totes Meer –
how can he fold into himself

all of this, and everything else
his selfish selfless self subsumes?

he watches a cleft in the rocks
where suds from each succeeding wave

hiss and vanish in their dying,
popping at the rim like whispers –

each time it's different, each time
exuberant bands bubble up

and blow their soft syncopations,
scarcely audible but freshly

conceived and individual,
not that hollow simulacrum

of the sea's noise a man might haul
away in the shell of himself –

it's as if the secret sources
of the sea wish it to be known

that each wave is a novelty –
its difference is its only truth –

though no new beauty rises from
the waves, naked and virginal,

seductive in its coils and curls,
those potent gods that hide within

the waves in microscopic swathes
of variation move like ghosts

among the rocks, reiterative,
original, mysterious

as stars – in wave on wave they make
their motives known, which are to be,

and be again, and endlessly
to be, so long as there are rocks

to dash upon, and winds and tides
and turbulence, and the earth's tilt –

the sea is drowning in itself –
to be lonely is to know its

separating shout, whether from
this shore or that unknown other

where a man mutters to himself,
checks his palisade, skims a stone

or two like liquid arpeggios
out to sea, primes his parakeet.

Wardrobe

The Ercol Windsor double wardrobe wouldn't fit
The place intended but if instead we stood it
In the gap behind the door and moved the bed
So that its head was by the window, then the dead
Space where her mother's ottoman had gathered dust
For years came into play. We'd get it in then, just.

But days brought dints and shuffling inconvenience
And all that 1950s elm wood elegance
Could not, we found, encompass every need, unless
We used the landing to undress, ignored the mess
Left bundled by the bed, and took the nagging draught
Around our heads as what you get for choosing craft.

Fine joinery enjoins us to enjoy, but joy
Endured in sleeplessness is seldom unalloyed.
A bed abandoned cools and leaves that rumpled space
Where all the shelved ideas and mutinies embrace.
The other room becomes the other man, and he
Has walk-in wardrobes deep and dark as destiny.

Krazy Kat

Ignatz, my little mouse, my love,
I have no longing for the world.
My dreams are of black skies and bricks
  Lovingly hurled.

My little one is locked away.
Where in the world my love can go
Only the wild desert flowers
  Grow up to know.

The dumb opuntia in its pot
Knows more of love's touch than I do.
It spikes and lives. It goes without
  As I do you.

The world keeps changing, frame by frame.
Order is the rule of a stick,
And love a new blow to the head
  With an old brick.

Blind Man's Buff

When some well-meaning but ultimately
Uninvolved person like myself asks them
How they are – Amy, Ellie, Hatty and Jack –
They each look back and say, Yeah, I'm OK.
Young people, pleasant and polite, well brought
Up, attractive, bright, and utterly broken.

A coastal fog has settled on their view.
Compression, as of flowers in a book,
Has fixed them and their features to a page
Of perfect emptiness. The game's begun
And they are in the middle, blind and beaten,
Fumbling for the noise of others' fun.

The Edge

Chardin was discreet; a sprig of herb
Or coil of kitchen twine, an angled knife
Or curlicue of peel, some dead, recumbent
Animal, scenting the dark, is all that he allowed
Beyond the edge of his plain stone ledge.

Only in his larger pieces, such as the grand
Oval of seventeen sixty-four with hanging duck,
Does he permit the folds of linen to cascade,
In starchy imitation of the mallard's situation,
Which is grave, and on which gravity all depends.

It's partly the disposition of things in space.
If the edge lies too high up the picture plane
It leaves a gap that needs explaining to the eye
With drapery or fruit, some fulsome rose that blooms
Against the gloom, a curious snail or pendant plum.

Zurbaran was bold. His famous canvas is unusually wide.
The elements declare their ordered artifice
By lining up symmetrically and, in the foreground,
The umber table edge runs unbroken for the full width.
It is the world as God might have painted it,

Measured, laid out on silver salvers with a certain
Fussiness to get it right, a feng shui arrangement
Of forbidden fruit, a plucked rose and a coffee cup,
Posing like a question in that elevated space beyond
The edge that marks the separating void, our void.

Weir Gate

There were three kids
and two were friends
and one was no friend
to either but, abject in
his hope, just tagged along –
and one warm after-school
afternoon they dawdled,
one behind the other
two, whose hum was
like the company of bees,
they dawdled all three
through the thoughtless town
and the groups of mothers
intimate in talk, and
the boarded shops
and the struggling trees,
the two in friendship
fixed on finding roadside
stones that were of use,
the other just a yard
or two behind, testing
each insinuating step
like warming for audition,
twirling and turning,
skipping over cracks,
swinging around lamp posts
with that stiff insouciance
that is the fixed face of
aching need – in such
a manner all three
wandered home without
a hint of guile or
obvious malintent,
away from the suburban
streets, the plots of

tended grass and
flowering privet,
and took a turn without
a word being said along
a path that led them
through a threadbare copse
of sycamore and elder,
fly-tipped refuse,
spindle and dogwood,
to that private place
of privilege and
childhood dereliction
the one who followed
knew about by word but
had no claim upon –
a dark ammoniacal
den of wood rot
and shards, discarded cans
and sins unspoken in the
spirit of enquiry, where,
among the cigarette butts
and bottle-glass,
the dampened ashes of
an old illicit fire
and items of a
girl's clothing left
limp on a stump,
a peevish instinct
ruled, a petty god
whose fondness was for
rupture in the world –
and his throne was a
barked log and his anthem
was the saw-sharpening
song of the great tit
and the moonlit yowl
of an occasional fox –

and hard by was a
river with a weir gate
and a swing that flew
over it, a crapulous
contraption of old
rope and pallet wood
and cankerous knots,
hanging slantwise and lax
above the giddy water –
and malice loured there
like nimbus on that
hot June afternoon,
ready to discharge,
and in its swelter
the goblins of the wood,
whose underlings were
clubs and knucklebone,
whose eyes were in the
fissures of the oak gall,
whose cronies were the
ivy and the clematis,
the bloodless lichens
and the silent moss,
the goblins took from
codices of stone
a message of derision
for the sun god, a
mucous scrawl of rambling
chants, a statement of
the wood's antipathy
to light and light's source,
and hummed it like
a memory of home
or distant drone
of car tyres on tarmac –
and with the sullen spite
of summer idling in

their blood, the two who
were friends turned upon
the third, who had no
friend to call upon,
and made him strip in
honour of initiation
and, like frenzied
puppeteers, cast him
clinging to the swing,
flying and twisting
out above the cabled
waters of the weir gate
and later left him there –
and while the two went
home and watched and
ate whatever was their
favourite, the other kid
was ragged about
abominably all night
like some maniacal dancer
in the final flood.

Nuthatch

For ten days or so
The nuthatch made the
Nesting box its own

And the air, which was
Particularly
Promising that year,

Was full of his weep
Weep weep weep weep – an
Anthropomorphic

Rendering, I know,
But birds, I like to
Think, feel sorrow too.

Things were going on –
A suicide who
Died and then survived,

Solemn as a church,
A dozen lonely
Kids and some whose lives

Were like a punishment;
One who hated love
So much she tried to

Mutilate herself.
I didn't notice
When the nuthatch went.

Days of words went by
With no solution.
When at last the loss

Of that acerbic
Song cut through the silence
Of a flat impasse,

She and I both bored
Of truth and bored
Of words and lies,

No salutary thought
Came with it. The air
Had warmed, was less chaste,

Leaf-burst had advanced
And now the blow-dried
Bulkiness of the

Tree tops I could see
Had the fluttering
Fashion of summer,

A factual and
Insistent fullness
That was saddening.

The failure of the
Nuthatch – I assume
He'd failed – didn't feel

Like revelation,
Not to me, at least.
The girl, who knows

What she'd have thought?
Mysterious words
Of chanting childhood

Came to mind unbidden –
Supernal, coeval,
Simony, succour –

Words that meant nothing
Then and nothing much
Now, holes in meaning

Where some meaning was
Intended, words I'd
Hoped to understand

One day, when I was
Older and knew the
Things that adults knew.

Two Rivers Press has been publishing in and about Reading since 1994.
Founded by the artist Peter Hay (1951–2003), the press continues
to delight readers, local and further afield, with its varied list of
individually designed, thought-provoking books.